PEGGY'S SCRA

Lucas Books

PEGGY'S SCRAPBOOK

Cooking and other Household Hints

by Peggy Cole

First Published by LUCAS BOOKS 2006
ISBN 1903797-55-1
EAN 9781903797556

Copyright Peggy Cole 2006

Printed in the UK by Winsor Clarke Brackenbury Ltd

CONTENTS

COOKING TIPS

We all have days when everything seems to go wrong. Here are some of my tips to rescue the disasters.

Apples

Next time you bake apples, stuff a piece of peppermint rock (candy stick) into the cores and bake as usual. The candy melts and gives the apples a wonderful flavour.

Apples make a nice drink. Try this Apple Toddy. Take 2lb apples, peeled and sliced; the juice of two lemons; 3 tablespoons of honey and $1/2$pt. water. Cook the apples with water until soft. Strain and stir in the honey and lemon juice. Take hot for colds and sore throats.

Apple Tart

To improve an apple tart, try sprinkling 2-3 tablespoons of orange juice over the apples. This gives a delicious flavour to improve the apples if they sometimes have no taste.

Aubergines

This vegetable should always be sliced, tossed with salt and left to drain for 1/2 hour to let bitter juices escape before cooking. Wipe dry with clean cloth or kitchen towel.

Avocados

To stop them from discolouring, brush them when open with lemon juice.

Baking

Put a shallow dish of water in the bottom of an oven to stop cakes from burning. This is particularly useful when leaving a rich fruit cake to cook unattended and it also seems to help to produce a moister cake.

If you are short of eggs when making a rich fruit cake, at least one egg can be replaced with a tablespoon of vinegar. Surprisingly it adds a very good flavour to the cake.

To stop cherries sinking to the bottom of a cherry cake, add a pinch of cream of tartar to the flour.
Arthritic hands may find that mixing cakes and puddings is easier if it is done in a saucepan which can be held by the handle, rather than in a bowl.

Bananas
You can freeze bananas. I know the skins go black, but the insides are quite all right.

Beetroot

As soon as it is cooked allow the cold tap to run over it for a few seconds, then rub the beetroot gently in the hands. The skin will soon come off.

Biscuits

We often get broken biscuits in our tins. Try putting them in the food processor. They will make a good base for cheesecakes. All you need is 8oz. sweet crumbs, 4oz. melted butter and 1-2 oz. sugar. This will make an 8-9 inch base.

Boiled Bacon

Once I have boiled a bacon joint I like to leave it in the water that it has cooked in. This will keep it moist and succulent.

Bouquet Garni

I find this is a nice gift to give friends who don't grow their own herbs. All you need is a small square cheesecloth. Place in it a bay leaf, a sprig of parsley and a sprig of thyme. Tie with a piece of ribbon. It's so easy to tie on the handle of a saucepan or casserole when cooking.

Bread

I hate waste so when I get bread that has gone stale I sprinkle it with water, wrap it in kitchen foil and place it in the oven, 425°F or gas mark 7, for 5-10 minutes. Or you can put it in a food processor to make crumbs for all sorts of uses.

Brown Stock

When making stock from meat bones, brown them under a hot grill or in a hot oven and then the stock will have a deep, rich colour.

Butter Beans

When you need to soak a few for stews, etc, do a large bag at a time then you can freeze them. It's so handy when you want to make up a casserole. You just take a few out of the freezer.

Cakes

Sometimes our cakes don't cook successfully. What do we do? In the past I have put mine in a trifle. I have also put orange juice over half the cake and put it in a basin to steam it for one hour. Serve with cream.

Cheese

When cooking with cheese, use a strong one and you won't need as much. Don't let cheese boil or it will go stringy. If you get leftover pieces of cheese, grate them and store in the fridge. This will come in handy for soups or pasta dishes.

Cider

When cooking with cider do not use an iron or tin pan as it will turn the cider black. Use an enamelled or porcelain lined pan instead.

Cure for a Cold, a real Suffolk Remedy

Take one large Spanish onion. Cut it up and cover with 2 tablespoons demerara sugar. Place in a soup bowl until clear. Take one tablespoon of the juice three times daily.

Curries

If you make a curry dish too hot, add some natural yoghurt, soured cream or potato.

Evaporated Milk

When whipping evaporated milk, add icing sugar, one tablespoon to one large tin. This keeps the milk frothy and makes it taste like fresh cream.

Eggs

When boiling eggs, put a spoonful of vinegar to the water. This makes them shell more easily.

Fish

Nobody loves the smell of fish cooking. You can wrap it in foil and bake it. Herrings will cook well in this way. Many of us like to fry sprats and herring. Just dust with fine oatmeal and sprinkle the frying pan with salt. Don't put oil in the pan, as the salt will draw the fat from the fish.

Fried Bread

For really crisp fried bread, dip each side of bread very briefly in cold water before frying. Toasted bread is also delicious fried.

Fruit

Peaches and tomatoes peel easily if put in a bowl of boiling water. Count to 15 before removing.

Frying Bread

Moisten it first with milk. It fries better and saves fat.

Game or Poultry

When you are about to pluck game or poultry, first immerse the bird in boiling water for about one minute. This makes plucking easier and avoids the problem of fly feathers.

Garlic

Garlic juice is an antiseptic and was used in the First World War to clean wounds.

Herbs
To make herbs last longer, chop fresh herbs and freeze in plastic cups. Use them frozen.

Ice cream
If you want quick ice cream, take half a pint of double cream. Whip until stiff then fold in a one pound jar of apricot jam and freeze. No need to beat as it freezes well.

Jam

1. Clip a clothes peg on to the handle of the wooden spoon and lodge it over the edge of the pan to prevent the spoon falling in.

2. Add a knob of butter to boiling jam and it will help to prevent scum forming. Allow jam to cool off for a few minutes, then stir well before pouring and scum should disperse.

3. When making plum, damson or bullace jam, cook the fruit until soft and allow to cool. Then, wearing gloves, it will be much easier to pick out the stones than by catching them in a spoon in the usual way. Finish cooking as usual.

4. Once jam or marmalade is cooked, I stand my pan in cold water for 10-15 minutes to let the fruit settle. If you don't let it stand, you will find that the fruit floats to the top of the jar.

5. Don't make jam with over-ripe fruit as you will find it will be a job to get a good set. Under-ripe fruit makes the best jam.

Lettuce or Parsley (or any green leaf)
These keep fresh and crispy for up to three weeks if you put them in the fridge in a large polythene bag loosely tied at the top.
Don't break up a lettuce before serving it as the leaves will go brown in the fridge. Never cut a lettuce, pull it apart.

Left-over Cheese
Put equal quantities of cheese and left over crusts of bread into the food processor and crumble them all up together. Freeze in a plastic bag and use as required as a topping for fish or pies, etc.

Mustard
Try making up mustard with sherry when serving it with roast beef or steak and kidney pie.

Nuts
Soak walnuts overnight in salty water. It is easier to crack the shells without smashing the contents.
Store nuts in the cool.
For Brazil nuts, put them in water brought to the boil for one minute, plunge back into cold water and you will find they will shell more easily.

Pasta, Rice and Potatoes (or indeed anything that needs a full pan of water).

These will boil contentedly without boiling over if a few drops of cooking oil are added to the pot. The oil breaks the surface tension of the water.

If your cooked pasta is sticky, rinse quickly with boiling water, drain and toss in olive oil or butter.

Party Sandwiches

If you need to make up a large quantity, a sandwich loaf of $1^3/4$lb will yield 22 slices and requires 4oz soft butter or margarine. An unsliced bloomer loaf yields about 16 slices and requires the same amount of butter as a sandwich loaf. A French stick 20 inches long yields 20 slices. Also 24 bread rolls require 7oz butter or margarine.

To go with the sandwiches:
When making tea:
30 cups: 50g tea; $1/2$ litre milk; 5 litres water
110 cups: 200g tea; 2 litres milk; 18 litres water

When making coffee:
50-55 cups: 450g ground coffee or 75g instant; 4 litres milk; 6 litres water.

Pastry

For an extra light pastry, add a little lemon juice to the water when mixing.

Potatoes

Before scraping new potatoes, leave to soak for five minutes in hot water with a pinch of bicarbonate of soda. The skins will come off easily.

Scotch Eggs

Add a handful of white breadcrumbs ($^1/_2$lb) to the sausage meat when making Scotch eggs. It makes the sausage meat go further.

Stews or Soups too Salty

Add 2 or 3 sliced, peeled potatoes to the liquid. Simmer for ten minutes then remove the potatoes. If still rather salty blend in a little milk or cream as this absorbs the flavour.

Sweetcorn

If cooking sweetcorn cobs, don't add salt until they are cooked as the salt toughens the kernels.

Textured Sponge

A tablespoonful of hot water, beaten into sponge mixture last thing, will greatly improve the texture of the cake.

Storage Life for Cooked Food in the Deep Freezer

Bread rolls	12 months
Bread	12 months. Very good sliced, toast from frozen state.
Dough	Only 1 month (as loss of yeast after then)
Small cakes	Creamed mixture: 6 months
Small cakes	Unbaked: 2 weeks
Large cakes	6 months (sponge/Madeira type)
Fruit pie, baked	6 months
Fruit pie, unbaked	2 months (better result)
Scones	12 months (heat to thaw)
Stews	6 months
Soups	6 months, condensed very good
Crab and lobster	1 month
Potato croquettes	2-3 months
Meat joints	12 months
Sandwiches	1 month

Fish, white	3 months
Fish, oily	24 months
Most vegetables	1 year (also fruits)

RECIPES

Million Pie

Cut a ripened marrow into slices. Add sugar and whole raisins. Put marrow in a dish with water and sugar and cook in oven until quite tender. Cover with a pastry crust. Sometimes the pie was left open with pastry criss-crossed on top.

This dish was eaten at Sunday dinner in winter. Sometimes it was made with pastry on the bottom. The marrow was beaten with egg and poured into the pastry case. This was called Million Custard.

Tuna Mousse (serves 4)

1 x 6$^1/_2$ oz. can tuna in water, drained
2 eggs, beaten
$^1/_2$ pt. milk
4 oz. Cheddar cheese, grated
4 tablespoons mayonnaise
1 stick celery, finely chopped
salt and pepper
fingers of toast, lemon wedges and parsley to serve
Pre-heat oven to gas mark 2 / 300°F / 150°C
Mash tuna in a basin. Then add eggs, milk, cheese, mayonnaise, celery, salt and pepper. Mix thoroughly.
Place mixture into four buttered ovenproof dishes and smooth the tops.
Bake for approximately 40 minutes.
Serve hot or cold, garnished with a lemon wedge and sprigs of parsley on each, with fingers of toast.

Mrs Farrant's Apple Cake

8 oz. self-raising flour
4 oz. sugar
3 oz. butter, chopped into cubes
3-4 Bramley apples, chopped into cubes
1 beaten egg and milk
dried fruit and nuts

Mix together. This looks nothing like a cake – more like a batter with lumps in it.
Bake in a well greased dish for approximately 45 minutes at 170°.
Half-way through the cooking time, cover with greaseproof paper and sprinkle cake with sugar when cooked.
This is not a cake for slimmers! For a diabetic version, try using wholemeal flour, Flora Buttery and Dietade Fructose.

Onion Cough Recipe

Dice one large onion.
In a container such as a jam jar, cover the base to about $1/4$ inch deep with good quality brown sugar.
Then add a similar thickness of the diced onion, followed by another layer of sugar. Repeat these layers until you have used the onion and finish with a layer of sugar.
This should be left for 3 to 4 days, until the sugar has liquefied. Strain off the sugar into a second container and warm gently on a low heat or in a bain-marie.
Stir in an equal amount of honey and continue warming and stirring for five minutes.
Remove from heat and stir for 1 to 2 minutes as the mixture cools. The syrup is now ready.

This is delicious as it is but it can also be added to other medicines as a sweetener. For colds try it in an infusion of peppermint, yarrow and elderflowers.

Bacon Pudding

8 oz. flour
4oz suet
8 oz. bacon, chopped
1 large onion, chopped
mixed herbs

Mix ingredients together to a soft mix but not too wet.
Put into a greased pudding basin.
Steam for $2^3/4$ to 3 hours. Serve with gravy and vegetables.

HOUSEHOLD HINTS

Baths

Treat stains on enamel baths by rubbing salt with a soft cloth dampened in white spirit, vinegar or paraffin.

Bicarbonate of Soda

I always keep a large drum of bicarbonate of soda in my cupboard. It's one of the best and safest substances you can have around the home. Bicarb is an abrasive and a deodoriser and it cuts through grease. You can wash out the inside of a fridge with a solution of 1 tbsp. bicarb to a pint of water. Ovens can be cleaned (that are not too dirty). Wipe the surface first then sprinkle it on and rub with a metal or nylon scourer. If you burn a saucepan, leave some bicarb with warm water in it to soak overnight. Next morning a good clean with a scourer will clean the burn marks off.

Brass
Lemon juice mixed with Brasso not only makes the brass brighter but delays the tarnishing process.

Brazil Nuts
Put in the freezer for several hours before shelling. When you crack the shells, the kernels will come out intact almost every time.

Candles
The simplest and easiest way to fit a candle to a candlestick is to dip it into hot water. Candles improve with keeping, left exposed to the air for a few months. The wax hardens and will burn longer and brighter.

Carpets
(1)   To remove a dent made by furniture in the carpet, place an ice cube in the dent overnight to bring up the pile.

(2)   To remove wax, oil or grease, from a carpet iron through blotting paper and rub off with turpentine on a clean rag.
Treat burns on a carpet immediately, by rubbing over affected area with a slice of raw potato.

China
Lime lines on glass and china can easily be removed by rubbing them gently with a soft rag soaked in cider vinegar.

Clean Wallpaper
This is an old and effective method for cleaning fingermarks and light stains. Get some bread, almost stale but not totally bone dry. Rub the crust over fingermarks. You will be surprised at how clean it comes up.

Colds
To relieve a stuffy head cold, place a saucer of chopped onions by the bedside.

Duvet Covers

When drying duvet covers hang them on the line inside out to prevent the sun from fading them. Also when you put a clean cover on the duvet, remember it's easier if you turn it inside out.

Flasks

When storing a vacuum flask put a lump of sugar in it to keep the flask fresh smelling.

Freezers

After defrosting a fridge or freezer wipe around the inside with glycerine on a rag. This will speed up the defrosting process next time.

Glass

When a glass gets broken, use damp cotton wool or bread to pick fragments up safely.

Ink Stains
Ballpoint pen marks on clothes can be removed with methylated spirits.

Labels
If you have stick-on labels which have all stuck together, they will separate easily if a warm iron is placed on them for a few seconds.

Net Curtains
Fold in a neat parcel and put in the washing machine. They will shake out without creases.

Onions
Old tights do very well for storing onions.

Orange Peel

Hang bags of dried orange peel round coat hangers in your wardrobe. Clothes smell great and keep moths away.

Parcels

Wet the string before tying up a parcel. As it dries it will become firm and taut, making the parcel more secure.

Polishing

Don't wear rubber gloves when polishing silver, as it will produce dark smears.

Polishing Silver

Rub your silver pieces with a soft woollen cloth dipped in methylated spirits. You can also remove blackened egg stains by plunging objects into water in which potatoes have been boiled. Dry carefully afterwards with a soft cloth.

Refrigerator Smells
To get rid of unpleasant smells, put a saucer full of charcoal in your refrigerator.

Tired Feet
If you've been on your feet all day, rub a little methylated spirit into the soles of your feet to revive them after a hard day's work.

Sellotape
A roll of sellotape that appears to be gummed solid will loosen if held over steam for a few seconds. Another handy hint I often use is to attach a paperclip or small button on the end of a roll of sellotape. It saves fiddling time.

Shoes
Don't dry wet shoes by the fire (we found this out in our young school days). Soaked leather, if dried quickly, will become brittle and cracked

and develop white "tide marks". The old way is still the best way. Stuff them with crumpled newspaper and leave to dry slowly and naturally.

Smooth Running Curtains
A little polish or Vaseline rubbed along a curtain rail will make the curtains pull across easily.

Stainless steel
Many items in the kitchen are made from stainless steel. These can be cleaned by soaking in denture powder and water, cheaper than commercial stainless steel cleansers. I use them in china teapots also.

Tar marks
Soak a piece of white rag in a little eucalyptus oil and rub it on the affected part until it is quite clean. This is suitable for delicate

materials. A tip for grass stains: wet with cold water, cover with cream of tartar, then if possible put it in the sun to bleach. Hot vinegar will remove paint stains.

Vinegar

My mother used a lot of vinegar for so many things. When she had a bad headache she would dip a large handkerchief in vinegar and tie it round the head like a bandage. If meat was giving off an odour, she would wash or soak it in vinegar. For slimmers, try some apple cider vinegar in a glass with honey and water. This is to take hunger pains away.

Windows

My mother always cleaned her window in this way – with crumpled up newspapers. Put in a bowl of tepid water with methylated spirits or vinegar, about 3 tablespoons to 4 pints water. Polish with dry newspaper.

AT THE SHOWS

HINTS FOR COOKERY EXHIBITS

Biscuits (a plate of six biscuits undecorated)
These should be small, not too thick and baked through so that they are crisp. Size, colour and shape should be even.

Bread Rolls
These should be even in size though not necessarily the same shape. They should be well risen and have a neat shape and appearance. They must feel light in relation to their size. They must not show signs of ugly kneading marks. If an egg glaze is used this should be applied carefully.

Fancy Biscuits

These should be more or less the same size, though not necessarily the same shape. Each one can be decorated differently. Tasteful colouring of the icing is important, and royal icing is better than water icing.

Gingerbread

This should be glossy and evenly baked with a reasonably flat top, no peaks or cracks. The whole slab should be shown unless the schedule states 'pieces'. A slab is usually about 10" x 6". It really should taste of ginger. Sometimes fruit and/or nuts are included in the recipe.

Jam Tartlets (Short crust pastry)

Pastry should be about one-sixth of an inch thick and tartlets should not be too deep. The texture of the pastry should be crisp and 'short' in the mouth, not hard or brittle, and the colour should be a light golden brown. The jam should be a smooth level layer and all the tartlets should be a uniform shape, colour and size.

Jam Tart on a Plate

As above, but the edge may be decorated to give the double thickness, e.g. tiny cut out pastry shapes, scalloped or fluted. The edge should not be too wide in relation to the size of the tart. A thin lattice of pastry may be arranged over the jam, but most important, the bottom pastry should be quite cooked and crisp under the jam filling.

Madeira Cake

This cake should be a pale golden brown. The top should be slightly domed and almost free from cracks. The sides should be straight with a thin golden crust on both sides and tops. The texture should be even and fairly fine, not close or tight, and there should be no disfiguring cake rack marks on the bottom. The flavour is, of course, very important. Sometimes lemon is used, sometimes vanilla.

Plain Fruit Cake

A domed but not pointed top is desirable, some slight cracking is permissible but there should not be any burnt fruit on the surface. Inside the cake the fruit should be evenly distributed. Other points as for Madeira Cake.

Plain Scones

The size, shape and colour should be uniform. They should have a smooth finish and be unglazed. 2 – 2½" is a good size for round scones. They should be a pale golden brown and have a firm but springy texture when pressed between fingers. The flavour can usually be improved by a pinch of salt. They should not have sugar or fruit in, otherwise they really belong to "Sweet Scones" or "Fruit Scones" and should then have glazed tops.

Sponge Sandwich (Fatless Sponge)

A plain flour will give a closer texture to a sponge than self-raising flour but a more open texture is still acceptable. The colour should be pale golden brown. The thickness of each layer should be uniform and the tops should be level. It is best to bake in two tins otherwise the jam soaks in too much on cut surfaces. Too much jam should not be used and the cakes should be sandwiched with insides together.

Rich Fruit Cake (more than half fat to flour with corresponding amount of sugar and eggs)

The tops should be flat, or almost so. Fruit on the outside should not be hard or burnt. The fruit inside should be evenly distributed. The colour of the crust and crumb should be a rich dark brown, the crust should be thin and the texture fine and moist, not heavy, close or soggy. The cake should cut cleanly and not crumble.

Sponge Cakes

As for Sponge Sandwich, and the outside crust should show evidence of correct coating of tin (flour and sugar dusting over the oiled tin).

Shortbread

This should look smooth, neat, be evenly shaped and be of uniform colour. It should have a bright appearance, not look muddy or be overcooked at the edges. It is important that it is 'short' right through and that it has a good flavour.

Small Fancy Cakes

All must have a cake base. Assorted designs show more skill than a number all alike. A variety of decorating mediums may be used, e.g. cream, almond paste, icing, butter icing, etc. Also nuts, fruits like cherries and angelica may be used in a design.

The cakes should be uniform in size though not necessarily in shape. The quality of icing and butter cream is important, but flavourings should not be over emphasised, especially cocoa. Small cakes may be shown in paper cases but they need not have been cooked in them. There will no doubt be other items included on the schedule but most of the points dealt with here apply in one way or another.

Loaf of White Bread (Yeast Dough)

Note: A 1lb loaf means it should weigh 1lb after cooking. The shape and colour should be uniform and true to type. The underneath should be free from kneading cracks and be a warm golden brown colour. 'Oven spring' of tin loaves should be even. The bottom and edges of the loaf should be clean and the crust should be smooth, a crisp golden brown with no ugly cracks. When cut the crumb mixture should be light, fine and even, free from streakiness and holes. The flavour of the bread should be well developed and free of any suggestion of yeasty sourness.

The crumb texture of brown bread should be closer, moister and less springy to the touch than white bread.

HINTS FOR CHRISTMAS

When holding a party put cling film over your best polished table to avoid water or wine marks from glasses.

Candles
Cut down the smoke in the atmosphere by burning candles. Candles kept in the fridge for a few hours will burn more slowly.

Non-Alcoholic Drinks
A cheap and non-alcoholic drink for drivers is soda water with a slice of lemon and a few drops of Angostura bitters.

Red Wine
An inexpensive red wine, if left uncorked at room temperature for at least two hours, will improve in taste.

Icing

A teaspoon of glycerine added to royal icing stops it becoming too hard.

Nuts

Soak walnuts overnight in salty water. They will crack more easily without smashing the kernel inside the shell.

Always store your nuts in a cold place, as they become rancid extremely quickly if left in a warm atmosphere.

Christmas puddings

If you have not made your Christmas pudding, mix it with cold tea instead of beer as this gives a richer colour and stops it drying out. If by chance the pudding turns out like a cannon-ball, slice it and fry it in butter and serve with brandy butter or cream.

Left-Overs
The left-overs from the turkey seem to hang around for days.
Try this old recipe,
"A Wet Devil":
Take any pieces of cooked poultry, cover with mustard or any other pungent condiment and grill or heat in the oven. Make a sauce with roughly the following ingredients – the juice of a lemon, a little red currant jelly, cayenne pepper, 1 dessertspoon of white sugar, _ a teacup of wine and _ a teacup of ketchup or Worcestershire sauce and 1 teacup of gravy. Heat them together then pour over the dev-illed poultry and serve very hot.

Cold turkey, ham or any other poultry
can be put in the processor and mixed with a little salad cream or chutney, to be used as sandwich fillings.

Baked Potatoes.
Place in a hot oven for about one hour, cutting a cross on each with a sharp knife. Serve hot with strips of cold ham and turkey and a little chutney.

Bacon
To give that boiling bacon extra flavour, add 1 teaspoon of vinegar, 4 cloves and a little nutmeg to the water.

Almond paste left over from decorating the cake can be used for stuffed dates. Just take the stones from the dates and fill in with almond paste.

Brandy butter
served with mince pies or baked apples – it's surprising how long it will keep in an airtight jar.

Crystallized and glacé fruits

Whole or broken pieces can be used for cake decoration or toppings for ice cream. I also use stem ginger, chopped and mixed in with ice cream and a chocolate sauce.

Pudding Charms

If you forgot to put charms in your Christmas pudding, wrap them in tin foil and put in the pudding whilst it is still hot. The slits will soon close.

Candles Dripping

To prevent your Christmas candle dripping, put a little common salt round the top of the candle, before lighting. It should not drip at all.